fake Paul

for Ann-Marie,
Enjoy!

fake Paul

Kimmy Beach

KBeach
a+BEC.

TURNSTONE PRESS

fake Paul

Turnstone Press
Artspace Building
607-100 Arthur Street
Winnipeg, MB
R3B 1H3 Canada
www.TurnstonePress.com

Turnstone Press gratefully acknowledges the assistance of The Canada Council for the Arts, the Manitoba Arts Council, the Government of Canada through the Book Publishing Industry Development Program and the Government of Manitoba through the Department of Culture, Heritage and Tourism, Arts Branch, for our publishing activities.

Cover design: Tétro Design
Interior design: Sharon Caseburg
Printed and bound in Canada by Kromar Printing Ltd. for Turnstone Press.

Library and Archives Canada Cataloguing in Publication

Beach, Kimmy, 1964–
  Fake Paul / Kimmy Beach.

Poems.
ISBN 0-88801-308-6

  I. Title.

PS8553.E119F35 2005   C811'.6   C2005-900772-9

Cover photograph by Greg Gazin   greg@gadgetguy.ca

for Dawn Andrea Beach
1978–1998

Contents

fake Paul

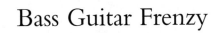

Bass Guitar Frenzy

Bass Guitar Frenzy

future mom
basement suite
my grandparents' home
nine February sixty-four

Ed Sullivan stooped   taut
wooden sweep of his right arm
Ladies and Gentlemen, The Beatles! Let's bring them on!
he introduces you
and all your lovin

George flirts
tilts his head forward   flashes his
uneven teeth to the camera at John's left

another camera finds a modest
white collar poking out at a throat
her hands out of her control
digging in her hair
tearing then flailing either side
her mouth   screaming

John sings, laughing, his face a little worried
girls in sweater sets scream, dance
precariously at the balcony's edge
a sea of fake pearls
cat's-eye glasses
one shrill voice calls *Ringo*

you play   cover your belly with
the body of your Hofner
studio lights ping from the guitar

this one   shaking her head along with yours
your *ahs*
wide white headband
in blonde hair
a man's silver ring on her right hand
checkered dress, dimples
her bangs graze her eyes
she falls back into
her chair   one hand
moves her laughing hair
left then right   she is overcome
her breath in little spurts
a sob now and again through tears

she knows that's how you would toss your head
while you made love to her
that stiff collar thrown to a corner
exaggerated head shake
a Blue Movie Star when he comes

~

you rarely look at the camera but once
you glance into my mother's eyes from
beneath a sweep of black brow

my mother sitting
on the scratchy brown of the old sofa
facing an oval black and white screen
of bobbing guitars
sweaty British temples and wrists
a sofa fragile with spindle legs
on protective foam disks
how she must have felt
that sofa shiver
in a bass guitar frenzy

~

the screaming peaks
wet studio seats, chair backs break
guards hold back girls
who know
in that moment love
will protect them when they
jump from the gallery to the stage below
    their love will keep them unharmed
when they fall before you looking for souvenirs
crushed jelly babies
drops of sweat

in the first balcony
a girl dreams herself
floating down to you before
she can be stopped
she throws one leg over the railing
her friends grasp at the edges of her skirt
tear at the hem as they try to catch her
swings her other leg over
and slips off the tarnished banister

below her, a sea of defiant teenage Beatle cuts,
waving arms, torn hair, front seats darkly empty
a surge toward four deep grey suits
black velvet collars
from up here she can see the seats
need repair   they creak and sigh into themselves
with each teenage bounce
such an old theatre
for such a boisterous show

dust in the deep amber and blue arcs
these old lights

so close now, her boys
so close   faces turned toward her
finally! she can see how you'd notice her
you won't forget her
the last face she will ever see

~

my mother watches, transfixed, a country away
nine months and one day later
I am born   neither early nor late

Lloyd's Copy of *Let it Be*

she pulls it from under a pile of beer bottles
holds it by a corner with her right
index finger and thumb
sour beer drips from the cover
my grandma hands it to me
nose wrinkled
here   you might like this longhair music
it's summer nineteen seventy-four
I am nine

take it from her hand
she moves away through the hall
bent grey over broom and dustpan
vacuum and Windex

the party last night so loud
I could hear it through the closed window
of my basement bedroom
wipe the album cover with the sleeve of my shirt

I like to stay over
help her clean up after parties in the hall she rents out
behind her west Edmonton house
I find cool stuff
key chains, empty bottles, money
but I've never seen anything like this
the bottom of the jacket is
so ripped I wonder how it hangs together
I hold the vinyl from below so it won't fall out

John got the worst of it
Lloyd stabbed across his head
in thick black marker
John's forehead obscured by a huge D
Lloyd set his beer
at the corner of the singing mouth
at the edge of John's angry eyes

I dismiss Ringo for the time being
the ridiculous moustache
red and white polka-dot shirt
sad-eyed stare   (I will love him, later)

charmed first by George's brilliant smile
he looks to his right to someone unseen
crisp collar, shaggy hair
gentle eyes laughing

above him, a man against a burgundy wall
eyes more brown than green
slim nose, messy hair
unshaven throat

I look up startled
to where grandma punches musty sofa cushions

the record is remarkably intact
Lloyd never called to see if he left it here?
I'll play it until he does

On Grandma's Couch

I am eleven when my wisdom teeth
are torn from my skull
mom ships me to grandma's for a week

grandma offers a book
for my convalescence
(The Beatles: A Rolling Stone Press Book)
and a sketch pad
never imagining the two would go together
some 4B pencils
a fancy art eraser

my week there spent in solemn
prepubescent contemplation
smudging Paul's eyes, mouth
a week of squirming
running thumbs over brows, jaw lines
digging my nails into the weakened paper
my frantic erasing
her cat twirling my ankles
grandma calls from the kitchen
she sounds like Mrs. Cunningham from the front of
the grade five art class I'm missing
don't get those shavings all over my rug
she brings me ice cream
as I blend and smooth
fingers black with graphite
tongue red with strawberries
from her backyard patch

Raw Hamburger

I'm not supposed to catch her
huddled over the green glass

each drawing earns her praise
though I learn her lack of passion
for my subject
she wipes her hands on the old
tea towel over her shoulder
and takes the sketch from me
with each new Paul head
she comments on my talent
how much it looks like him

she thinks I'm napping on her couch
the afternoon I catch her
a new Paul drawing slipping
from my sleepy hand
grandma's unruly grey hair
a hand to her mouth
fingers full of raw ground beef,
onions, eggs just beaten
she never uses a spoon to mix
her meat loaf
it just doesn't taste the same

a hand through it
squishing again and again
till her fingers go numb from
cold beef   whole handfuls to her lips
when no one is watching

I sit on the bar stool next to the counter
grandma offers a taste from her hand
the mass sticks to my tongue
raw egg strings down my throat
forbidden texture
fresh meat in my mouth
pepper   crunch of onion

I love the carnivore in her
the secret raw meat eater
inside her neat blue apron

Cancer Diet

she would go into the hospital saying
Come on kids, it's only cancer
Oh, cancer! we'd say
Grandma, you had us
worried for a second

that one about The Cancer Diet
you'd leave the hospital every time
at least five pounds lighter
what with that piece of calf removed
and then a breast
then half a lung
her favourite joke

when she died
we knew there was some mistake
knew she would climb out of bed
head out the door to church
slim and feisty as ever

At Your *Let it Be* Piano

Sound Check
[Studio Tour, Abbey Road, St. John's Wood, NW8, September 1983]

Brenda leans   thrums
the tops of cymbals over velvet ropes

I don't care who sees

me at your piano
I lean over the keys
run my tongue under
your microphone
take the dented head into my mouth
lick the shaft, its sharp sharp metal
lay my tongue flat
against its cold curve

sour stab at the back of my throat
your breath, hot smoke, beer
maybe you bumped it once
or twice with your lips
fucking the camera above
you with your eyes
the microphone swaying
me in my playing
an inch from your mouth
think of you moving
against the black wood
hard below the keys

with the tip of my tongue I poke
into the tiny holes
your microphone tasting
of words you must have left

Abbey Road Studios presents *The Beatles*

pumped up on spiked punch
stale chocolate-chip cookies
the day's food budget blown on
A Retrospective Beatles Film With
Music And Refreshments
two eighteen-year-old blondes
defying all *Do Not Touch!* signs

we climb forbidden stairs   fiddle with
antique knobs on old sound boards
reel-to-reel tapes
we look down from the booth
over the studio
a cute strawberry-blond boy takes a Polaroid of me
up through the window
we catch two
debutantes in sleeveless floral sundresses
one orange   one blue watching Brenda and me
their matching white
-gloved hands folded
over dainty British pocketbooks

afterward they will follow
us from a distance
to your house
wait to see what we'll do
hands folded tight
thighs pressed together

Paul,

I drop to my knees

with the edge of a thumbnail
carve your name into the soft
wood at the bottom of the door
I'm following you

#7 Cavendish Avenue
[London NW8]

crawl along the top of the stone wall
Brenda has given me a leg up
blood red door, clear transom
red garage left of the entrance
Paul McCartney's garbage
a black bag on the front stoop

how odd you would put your garbage out front
that you would *have* garbage at all
what the hell is in that bag? handwritten lyrics
to *Yesterday*? a lock
of your hair? Oh Christ

the breathless debutantes hang back
whisper behind perfect white hands
virgin voyeurs
they decide not to warn us of
the policeman's arrival
Brenda doesn't see him   she's looking
up at me breathless   *what else can you see?*

this bobby doesn't understand the depths
of our passion
our need to reach that garbage
rummage its secrets
then what?
demand entry?

he's not home, luv   the bobby calls up to me
he's in Scotland
you'd like to be arrested at his house
and him not even in it?

damn your logic!
I jump down
on your way, then

I tear a branch from the tree out front
wave it at the stiff-necked cop
we strut back to the tube at St. John's Wood
swishing past young skirts too afraid
to climb to the edges of things

Would you feel me?

[the next day, your house]

I just want another look around
don't want to be chased away
I was so rushed yesterday
and Brenda wanted to
stay in bed this morning

just so you know I'm not one of those
fucked-up types
the ones who camp in your driveway
lean against the brown metal gate
sing your songs off-key all night
shiver in rain waiting for your
car to leave or arrive
wet strays scratching to be let in
the ones who get further than I did
before they're caught inside
climbing feet first into ground floor windows
burying their faces in your pillow
stuffing your underwear into hot damp shirts
those girls are crazy

what do you *do* in there?
shave, sleep in
slouch about in stocking feet?
play with your sheepdog
write sheepdog songs
love your wife   her long blonde hair?

~

I'm just standing here at the gate for a moment
before I go
I know you're not home
I have to be someplace anyway

~

when you first get up   bare feet
padding down the creaky Victorian hall
your pajama legs draggling on
warped boards
into the cramped washroom
look at yourself in the discoloured mirror
you must touch the scar
along your upper lip
old surgery from a moped accident
(or was it that fight
with John? I've heard the rumour a
chivalrous defense of Cynthia earned you
a kick in the teeth)

ridge of uneven skin at the edge
of your mouth, still warm from sleep
is it numb? if I were to come
inside and lay my tongue against it
would you feel me?

1963–64

Oily Lace

[52 South Hunter Street, Liverpool, June 1963]

sky of brass
tarnished silver plate
identical rooftops snake
above twisting streets
greasy cobblestone and mould
chimneys in perfect rows
stab at gull shriek
curling smoke
cramped moist council homes below
boxes inside brick
petrol stink   sour cabbage

oily lace behind streaked
window glass   dusty plastic flowers
bleached on one side
sleeping in limp sun year after year

a middle-aged woman in a shapeless floral dress
pulls back the curtain
thick fingers   her wedding band
trapped by decades of skin
fragment of love long dead

she turns the handle of the rusted
can opener   scrapes cat food
into a dull metal bowl
the cat chews   lazy
same dinner day after day
he eats to please her

waiting for her water to boil
she bends to scratch the cat
just above his tail
he arches   she can hear him chewing
teacup to mouth to saucer
teacup to mouth to saucer

pads through the front room
peers out on the dim street
heads do not turn toward her
she switches on the telly   no one sees her
return to the brown recliner
its arms shredded by the old calico
that crawls into her lap
they settle in for *Ready, Steady, Go!*
     a bowl of milk
     a splash of brandy and tea

Upstairs

[Wavertree, Liverpool, 7:00 p.m., 03 August 1963★]

a bit more spray should hold it
it will be stifling down there
she finishes her homework early
the blue jumper just right
the pearls grandmum gave her
when she turned sixteen
they're not real but
he won't be able to tell

she'll be gone before they get home
they don't mind when she goes
to the lunchtime Cavern shows
they try to forbid her to go at night
but she's seventeen now   she'll go if she pleases
they worry about the kind of boys
she'll meet there   they don't know
there's only one who interests her

he holds his guitar
differently from the others in the band
his left wrist rubs the wood
slender fingers of his right hand at the strings
heels of his palms rough   calloused from months
of playing ten hours straight in dingy
German nightclubs
his eyes so big   tight leather trousers
just the sort of boy mum and dad
would be afraid of

★ the date of The Beatles' final performance at The Cavern Club in Mathew
Street, Liverpool

she avoids the creaky banister
though she's sure they're at the cinema
they'll stop at the Blue Angel for darts
and ale afterward
she's wearing her best black leather flats
comfortable but stylish

she's been saving her money
tonight she hires a taxi
no bus dirt for her

Love in the Best of Cellars

stone drips sweat and bitter
she pushes through   leans
against the wall on the right
tilts her head to the left so she'll fit
under the dripping arch nearest the stage
she's closer to him this way

tries to keep her hair in place but it's hard
with the damp smoke
her own heat
she knows all the words
makes sure she's singing
when he occasionally looks her way   winks
she's here every night
he must recognize her
navy blue jumper
blue eye shadow and fake pearls
she's heard *Some Other Guy*
a hundred times

he bounces on a wooden stage
so precarious his microphone stand sways
with each tilt of his hips
his feet trace the paint-chipped places
his own shoes have worn
on the hollowed wood

Behind the Cavern, 2:00 a.m., 04 August 1963

he finishes the last set, grabs
a Coke, wipes sweat from
his eyes   calls her
over to the stage
Bird! Aye, you!

smell of urine seeping
from filthy bathrooms
sinks into her jumper
he steps down from the low stage
John and George wipe moisture
and fingerprints from guitar faces
pack them in felt-lined cut-outs of themselves
Ringo tucks his sticks into their pouch
squints through smoke curling from his mouth
she moves through sticky
bodies to Paul's side
black hair plastered to his temples
one brow impossibly high
eyes on her breasts

move through soaking teenagers
blue heat of fetid arms, wet cotton
up top on Mathew Street
sweaty hand on her wrist
he tugs her playful into a doorway
stench of produce
heads of rancid lettuce at his feet
rats and silverfish

against the seeping brick
his wet leather rubs her
mouth hot on her
Relax, luv
she wants to

the Hofner bass he bought
in Hamburg left inside
while he makes her his
no one dares touch

Liverpool, December 1963

she's been to the doctor
no doubt now
can't go home
tries to go to school
sticks to dirty alleys at night
and the waterfront
she wanders down Bold
Street in the mornings   sleeps
at the YWCA in Rodney Street
her roommate Marion doesn't ask

Georgos' chip shop
is right over the road
she can get dinner for 6p
he watches her walk in each evening
now she watches him
smoke in a greasy apron
he leans on the plate glass across
from the dirty sill of her third-floor window
she can see the bald patch on the top of his head

from the other side of the room
in Hardman Street
she watches them building
the cathedral up on St. James Mount
they've been building it forever
a monster   unfinished, gaping
piles of red sandstone quarried in Woolton
waiting to be added to its
ridiculous bulk

Mike McCartney pulls lenses from a leather case
cameras   tripod
poses before the cathedral
different times of day or night
finds bits of weed-infested cement
at the base of the new red brick
white concrete twisted and mossy
left from a war just before his birth
he climbs them
takes his own picture
capturing darkness   shadow
rusted fences   maw of the open altar

she's taken some money from her father's wallet
and saved up the rest
enough to get her to America by boat
follow Paul to New York

~

Mike packs up his cameras
he's losing the light

APPLAUSE!

[*The Ed Sullivan Show,* CBS Studio 50, New York City, 09 February 1964]

i. A Dozen White Arrows

Thank you very much! Thank you!
Now yesterday and today our theater has been jammed

Ringo finds a comfortable position
and his stool gives a cracked vinyl creak
wipes his sweaty fingers on his trousers
palms his drumsticks

with newspapermen and hundreds of photographers

lick your fingers   smooth hair
over your forehead
tug down your jacket
hold a clean cuff over your left hand
wipe a fingerprint smudge from the Hofner's face

from all over the nation and these veterans agree with me

George clears his space
with the toe of his boot
likes to dance a little
during *I Want to Hold*
Your Hand   doesn't want to get tied
up in wires and microphone cords

that the city never has witnessed the excitement stirred
by these youngsters from Liverpool who call themselves
The Beatles.
Now tonight

you fuss with John's collar
straighten his tie
he bats your hands away
he wants to look a little ragged
wants you to quit
hovering like you're his mum

you're gonna twice be entertained by them:
right now, and again in the second half of our show.
Ladies and gentlemen,
The Beatles! Let's bring them on!

lights are on you
a dozen white arrows a dozen feet long
surround the four of you
pointing at your moving hips
nervous brows   Cuban-heeled boots

Close your eyes

ii. Mania

February 10, 1964. Tragedy struck last night in New York City as a young, pregnant woman was trampled by a group of youngsters caught up in what is being called "Beatlemania." The Beatles, the mop-top group from Liverpool, were making their first Stateside television broadcast last night on Ed Sullivan's popular CBS variety show.

Several fans of the Rock and Roll group were unable to obtain tickets to the live performance and became agitated on the street outside the studio. One unfortunate young woman (whose name has not been released pending notification of her next of kin in England) was trampled to death in the street. Her unborn baby was also killed in the melee. At press time, officials at CBS had not returned our calls.

~

they turn away as one crazed
organism with a single mind
find a television set in a storefront window
leave a bleeding girl on the sidewalk
casualty of this mania carried away
by ambulance
shadow of a child who will never be
floats over buildings, across oceans
          searching

a country away a young woman
in a small basement suite
feels a kick in her belly

Liverpool 2001

Ringo's Room
[10 Admiral Grove, The Dingle, Liverpool]

great sport, my husband
plodding with me through every
Beatles tour in Liverpool

this is where Ringo lived, honey
see the doll in the upstairs window?
that was Ringo's room

oh yeah? he says, tired
ready for a beer somewhere
he's finished taking pictures:
me in front of strangers' homes
they peer through blinds as bus after bus
stops before their house
they're just back from work
tired, they'd like to watch some telly
but the constant drone of the buzzer
makes them hang a sign
Please do not ring our doorbell
You cannot come inside to see Ringo's room
It's our daughter's room now

we ride down Penny Lane
in a conspicuous yellow
bus called *The Magical Mystery Tour*
I've seen it all before
barbershop, bank, roundabout
this church where John met Paul
John's preschool
the children's home hidden
behind iron gates at Strawberry Field

at the corner of Hope Street and Mount Pleasant
I ride out the last of the drizzly tour
high on Caffrey's Cream Ale
and the stench of sea
my hand on my husband's
thigh nudging
closer as we near our hotel

please do not disturb sign on our doorknob
one frilly single bed left empty
as he tries to thrust from me the memory
of tiny British postwar beds
sleepy with dark-haired boys
dreaming guitars

20 Forthlin Road

[Allerton, Liverpool L18 9TN]

we climb off the minibus   my legs
unprepared to be lost under me
a plaque to my right reads
The Property of
the NATIONAL TRUST
I stand in the foyer of the
tiny council house you lived in as a boy

my husband decides he doesn't want
to come in   he'll explore
the street where you lived
on the wall beside me
your brother's portrait
you standing in this doorway
the museum custodian pulls me
away from the group
we don't tell everyone this
he shows me the original
lino in the front hallway
I see where others have torn
bits from the lifting edges
shows me the floor in the kitchen
you've no idea how many Beatle
feet walked on these tiles
I kneel, my hands and mouth on cool ceramic

he's opening drawers, cupboards showing us
dishes and chipped cups the family
has returned to the house
I slip a tarnished steak
knife out of the silverware drawer
pocket it

he pulls an Oriental patterned tea tray from
behind the replica breadbox
this has been authenticated by Mike McCartney
Mary served the boys tea on this tray
after school every afternoon
he lets me touch it
my hands on warm black wood
I take the tray from him   hold it to me
run my fingertips over the faded dragon
at the centre   his fierce face scraped by
long-ago teacups and butter dishes
I see you in the parlour playing your first guitar
you take the offered teacup and a jam buttie
ta very much, mum
you are twelve   she
is still alive   the ache in her breast
won't take her for another two years

~

tiny front bedroom upstairs
brick pattern wallpaper
sleep and saliva on your pillow
I see you stumbling across the hall to
the w.c. in the middle of the night
your twelve-year-old feet padding
past Mike's room
pajama legs dragging on hardwood

now the door to your bedroom
hangs in a Hard Rock Café in London
open the replica door
a timid first girlfriend invited in while your dad
is at work selling cotton to wealthier
men's wives

I pull back the cream counterpane and crawl in
wet my face with your nighttime littleboy sweat
warm the bed for your return
cold toes   unwashed hands

Ferry Cross the Mersey

the cheery female voice tells me smuggling is
a high-risk crime and I hear *snuggling*
I am drunk on dark ale and salt

twice a day travellers must listen
to Gerry and the Pacemakers'
greatest hit
either side of me Liverpudlians creak
on benches   move
from Pier Head to Wirral
     and back
on their way to or from
work   the women pull their plastic bonnets
tighter around their faces
never fail to smile at me

behind me a black toque and a blue one
huddle inside thin jackets
I lamped that dodgy git good and proper. Smeghead
got on me tits.

a blond man in a long leather coat aims his
video recorder at me
May I film you, my love?
a hen party of cackling old women
poses for my camera

twined on a padded blue bench up front
in leather and tall hair
two teenagers recite the tourist message
along with the recorded voice
slipping in the odd *fucking*
or *smelly* when appropriate

a lanky brunette in a tight pink mac
passes the boys behind me   her cheeks rosy
with rain   her hips sway with the
boat's movement
she's carrying three beers

Phoar! Look at the talent.
I'd 'ave a go at that like, not 'alf! Feckin 'ell.
Nice gear that.

now the lilting voice
begins pointing out each landmark
I can barely make out the Liver Birds
atop the Royal Liver Building
shrouded in a hundred years of fog
one bird faces the sea to search
for lost sailors
showing them the way home
the other faces the city centre
one of the old women tells me
that one's looking
to see if the pubs are open
and even I know that's the oldest
joke in Merseyside

salt spray hits my cheeks
my husband waits for
me at the Pier Head   I waved
till I could no longer see him

a woman in a blue plastic mac
          weeps beside me
proper black pocketbook
in her lap   I imagine I am going
to work with her (or whatever
sadness she's approaching)

Yellow Submarine

step past the *Employees Only* sign
over piles of thick coiled rope
emergency door on the ferry's edge
lift the metal latch and let the heavy orange
door swing toward the seething Mersey
it's hard not to fall over the side
so I do

River Mersey is thick and brown
I see the concerned faces
of other passengers above me
waving through churning water
leaning over railings   calling me
calling one another
I hang below the surface
arms spread to keep me here

push down a few feet
at the river bottom a little city waits
everything is yellow and shiny
I can breathe

~

I once watched as a man I loved
snorted coke off the coffee table
I inherited from my grandmother
we were watching *Yellow Submarine*
his eyes glassy   my eyes on him
I was tempted   would have done almost anything
to prove I was cooler than his wife
white powder stuck in the tiny
grooves of the wood

after he left
I dug a little out of a groove
and rubbed it on my teeth
the way I'd seen them do it in the movies
a clean light passed over me
and I vomited
real Beatles on the screen now
holding cartoon props from the film
pretending they had something to do
with its creation

~

at this river bottom
Blue Meanies plan their next attack
Lennon's fantasies of Kinky Boot-Beasts
Apple Bonkers
Snapping Turks

replicas of you swim here and there
exaggerated cartoon sideburns
low languid eyes
you wave at me from a porthole
in a tiny submarine

a crowd gathers as I vomit
on the deck of the ferry
my clothes are dry
I look over the edge
yellow lights disappear
under the silt stirred up by rudders
you are waving up through water
propeller blades slapping

Underground:
[at The Beatles Story Museum, Albert Dock]

I've not told him I've left
him to find you
I seek you all ends of this rusting seaport town
row on row of compact cars
the dim, grimy morning
in Leece Street   St. Luke's church
bombed out and left as a reminder of a blitz
just before you were born
this spire   chunks of architecture
spit to the ground by the Luftwaffe
weedy granite behind metal gates
never repaired, never replaced
at protruding edges of this building
I stand on the front steps
a great chain across doors behind me
look down Renshaw Street   pungent noise of cars   shops

I turn left into Bold Street   its steep moist smells
exhaust   ripe fruit   jostled bodies singing
this street language
a fellow on the corner shouting
Get Your Big Issue!   Big Issue, my love?
I dig to find a pound   take the offered magazine
he calls to me as I leave   *I love you!*
across Church Street   Lord Street
right on South John and right
again into Mathew

tangle of wire and neon tubing
splinters of glass stick in the metal frame
Cavern   it used to say before a casual
wrecking ball crashed into it

this was never the Cavern
just some ordinary pub called that
back when everyone in Mathew Street
was calling everything The Cavern

Beatle Street

Four Lads
Who Shook
The World

garish statue hung high over
a warped, boarded door
the ruin of a faceless Madonna
holding three children's dolls
painted gold, heads thick with pigeon shit
the Lennon doll set apart
first to die

~

in The Grapes a darkened corner seat
aged green and cracking leather
a sharp black and white picture
you   Pete Best   George   John
drinking at this table
Oriental carpet   battered greens and blues
old smoke   orange leather on benches
that could have been stolen from a church
I order a white wine spritzer at the bar
sit in your seat
a blond man by the window takes
my picture   raises his pint toward me
I lift my glass to him   stroke this armrest

your fingers were here
sore from sweating on frets
five hours a night in the Cavern Club over the road
at the bar a drunken white-haired man sways
Don't you know who I am?
the bartender gives him a small bottle of merlot port
her hands steady on the beer taps
That's all for you, lad

I lean back   feel under
my table for sticky signs of you
dig my thumbnail into the soft wood
holding your hand sweat
I finish my drink   leave £2 on the table
for the John Smith Extra Smooth Ale I imagine buying you

~

into sunlight   right on Mathew Street to South
John Street left on Cook
cross over Castle to Brunswick Street
reach The Strand to Wapping
left past Canning Dock to Albert
Dock and underground
into The Beatles Story Museum

a wax statue of you in a fake
Abbey Road set holds a replica Hofner bass

collarless grey jackets
from *A Hard Day's Night*
your empty suit on the dummy
its brown wooden neck like a headless doll

swing my bare fist
punch a hole through glass
my hand goes numb   shards in the heel of my palm
I pull away jagged edges
toss them to the floor
push my arm through to reach your coat
tear it from the shoulders
the dummy thuds from the display case
bury my face in the jacket
my blood soaks your grey sleeves

        the must and ruin
haven't taken the sweetness
from this decaying fabric
I can smell you

Wax Head

The Beatles at Madame Tussaud's Wax Museum

[a Day Trip to Marylebone Road, London, June 2001]

i. beeswax fingers

shiny grey suits   beeswax fingers
replica guitars
you lounge across a red divan
clearly not meant for lounging
George leans against John's left shoulder
John's legs open, inviting
Ringo plays his right knee with sticks
Hofner bass across your thigh

troublemakers
longhairs

in Madame Tussaud's
secret underground laboratory
each human hair
is individually inserted into hollow
wax scalps glass globes
twisted into eye holes
seams smoothed away from
where the mould edges meet
wax hands and fiberglass arms
fitted into grey 1962 cuffs
wire torsos and legs attached
fingertips melted on guitar strings

leave my thumbprint on your wrist
lipstick smudge between knuckles

ii. in your lap

it's quiet in the museum tonight
nobody through this room
the last few moments
pry rubbery fingers from the Hofner
the heat from my hands
bends your wrists backward
your left hand comes loose!
lay it in Ringo's lap for now
Ringo can hold your guitar too

climb into your fibreglass lap
your body collapses beneath me
wire frame crumples   beeswax softens
between my thighs

Ringo shivers
his frozen face turned away
he won't embarrass us

take your left hand from
Ringo's lap
both your hands on me

iii. knapsack

if I can get this collar undone—

(how did she do it in Hamburg
back room of Der Kaiserkeller?
the tall German groupie
ten years your senior
she couldn't get at you
fast enough
your barely legal-age Scouser thighs
shoulder blades   she must have
torn the tie from your throat)

—I can see how this head is
attached   melted to your torso

I dig in my bag   find the McCartney
family knife   take your left hand
make a cut through your neck
slash your head off
pull it off in my hot hands

into my knapsack with you, Paul's wax head

iv. Mary's Bed & Breakfast, South Hunter Street, Liverpool

I've taken the top room
in this row house bed and breakfast
cold water sink
bathroom two floors down
sloped ceilings, a single bulb burns
at the apex   my view
is the top room
of the boarding house over the road

bangers, eggs, mash and toast
clothesline saggy with
yesterday's table cloths, napkins tossed
beside Mary's grandmother's plates as tourists
race out the door to see Liverpool

Mary, the proprietor, thick-legged
in a greasy floral print
her sunglasses on always,
scrapes fat into a tin can
bones creaking as she
pulls the bag from the morning
dustbin rays of smoggy sun
through splattered windows

make a deal with Mary
pay cash   stay as long as I like
no questions asked

v. pink chenille

when I don't return tonight
to the hotel room I share
with my husband
I suppose he might be
worried   he loves me
his hand on
the phone calling

the police   Paul, I take your
head from my knapsack
my hands on either cheek
set you down on my pillow
turn down rank pink chenille
pull the chain that dangles from the grimy bulb
on Mary's water-stained ceiling

vi. melting

you're not quite right
left eyebrow too high
eyes a bit glassy

I can fix you, love
they're amateurs
don't know what you *really* look like

in the morning
I'll light a white candle
hold your head over it
shape your face

lie with me tonight
burn between my thighs
I hold you either side of your face
my hands tangled in your hair
while you love me

wax lips melt me
I shudder   pull you to my mouth
clover blossom honeybees
your lips unrecognizable
a smear on your hollow skull

Sgt. Pepper's Wax Funeral

i. yellow hyacinth

I step over a red *B* of flowers
kiss your wax lips
you stand circa sixty-three looking
down into a grave containing
a left-handed Hofner
of yellow hyacinth

I don't want anything here
not even a flower from your bass
just you   but you
are connected to the others
right hand sewn to
Ringo's sad shoulder

I have to get in beside you
shove cardboard Oscar Wilde over
Tom Mix and Marlon Brando domino backward into
Stu Sutcliffe Mae West whoever
the fuck else is back there

I cut your hand free from Ringo's suit
the other pulls easily from your sleeve
drop them to the floor   push
George   John   Ringo forward
into the makeshift grave
they land face down
in dirt their feet broken off
shoes still attached to the floor

it's just you and me now baby
I take a bite from your left cheek
roll the cool wax on my tongue
my left hand inside your trousers
knife hangs at my right side
I swallow the wax lump

let you go
          topple
join your friends

ii. you   decapitated

on the other side of the studio I see
the white Austin Mini on a doll's little knee
outta my way, Marlene Dietrich
move it or lose it, Shirley Temple

this is the car they say you died in, Paul
driving around London at night
nineteen sixty-six, your head
torn free at impact
replaced by a perfect
doppelgänger with a scarred lip
the greatest cover-up in
Rock and Roll History

where did they take your head?
did they preserve it in some chemical
to keep it from decaying?
I'd love to have it but

I'll take the car from this doll's knee
wax ball hot in my gut

step over hyacinth crushed
beneath the weight of wire
bodies wax necks   stiff soft arms

Mary's Ointment

I think
my husband has gone home
I left him a message at the hotel
Go Home   it said

the McCartney roses I watered
in Mary's back garden aren't cooperating
I don't know why they won't bloom
I tear them out bare-handed
toss them over the fence

Mary's ointment will take care of it
a few wilted buds land on dirt
a little blood   that's all

52 South Hunter Street, L1 9JG

Piss off, you tosser! knocks me from sleep
a cascade   river of drunkspeak
ten minutes after twelve
my window open to the street
any breath of air
no matter how stale how ale
-soaked beer bottle smash   bits of glass lost
cracks between cobblestones

below my window a boy sits drumming his
palms on the wobbly metal table outside
the closed café   tick tick tick   high
heeled boots   lilting speech toward him

Oi! My love! You calling round tomorrow night?
Na   she says   *I'm skint, me*
impossible heels click   uneven stones
she and her friend pass the pub
voices moving up moving around
corners   moving down steep
streets to the river Mersey
her breathy laugh moving my curtains

squeal of brakes   two thirty-six
late night fight   two boys at it
around the corner in Maryland Street
sirens long low trucks
turning cars constant slam heavy
doors through thin walls
a toilet flushes
         the night moves on pacing itself
tries to hold all the noise it possibly can

ten to three   a spill of bottles crashes
into a bin in the alley back of the pub (faint
music three blocks away)

twenty-one minutes after three   a spill
of bottles crashes into a bin
in the alley back of the pub
(my face to the wall   hands over my ears)

three forty-seven
aspillofbottlescrashesintoabininthealleybackofthepub
(and my head leaves my body, floats over the great
green Liver birds to the relative
cool and quiet of the Mersey)

four thirty   ravenous street
cleaner makes three passes
down South Hunter Street
yellow flashing lights seek openings in my
thin blue curtains   bits of glass tinkle
knocked aside   great rotating brushes
maw of moving steel teeth   its nightly feeding
burrow into my pillow
in my mind I pace window to door
to bed to window to door to bed
to window   to window

quarter-to-five car alarm
someone walks too close from Kiss the Red
Pub and Billiards over the road
angry screech bounces
          more sirens
I crawl out of my small bed   part the curtains
angry neighbours in robes stand
in windows hold shutters open
Shut it! punches
the early eastern blue in its belly

five sixteen   bottle truck arrives
two long tusks up front stab through
metal handles on each bottle bin
long slow spill of green
amber   clear glass
each bin empties its coffin of glass
into the truck's moving graveyard of glass
seven bottle bins full with glass
          crunch and shatter
     spill and smash
each bin clanged heavy on cobblestone
empty shards rolling   sticky sweet beer

stench of bin bottoms
thick smell reaches me
the truck speaks   *Attention!*
This vehicle is reversing!

the beast extracts its tusks
its meal complete
makes its thick glassy way
toward Rodney Street
good thick English ale dripping
from its great heaving body

I crawl back in
sink into predawn half-dreams   crashing
cars   severed heads

glass and blood
    everywhere

The Cavern Club

I cross over Mathew Street
through the ten-at-night stick of sweating locals
tourists   low-cut tops and high high heels
drizzled damp and echo on a hundred wooden stairs
curling   descending into The Cavern Club
(a fake Cavern   the original
up the street bulldozed
a shopping centre, underground train,
two cafés in its place)

in this replica cave
a fake Beatles band under stone
bounces *Please Please Me* off thick wet walls
dancing bodies   pumping speakers
the Paul is right-handed
he doesn't look at all like you

condensation   sweat   love
drip on me from the rounded ceiling
turn my face to it
moisture runs down my neck
soaks into my collar
the band shakes the room
the stage pounding
my wineglass on the speaker
vibrates toward the edge with each
kick of the bass drum
a ripple of wine spiralling from the centre

a man in a long leather coat
takes my picture from behind a stone arch
his pint of Fosters on a small shelf at his elbow
he moves to dance behind me   his chin at my shoulder
his breath moves my hair

we dance at the side of the stage
walls rattle
noise and stink of too many people
too much ale
music too loud
I am so high

      so deep

underground

the Fake

Opening Night:
Linda McCartney's Sixties **Photo Exhibition**
[Provincial Museum of Alberta, Edmonton, November 2001]

i. Mad, Mad Modes for Moderns

the invitation says *dress up sixties*
everyone will go hippie
I decide to go mod
become a cartoon feature from
Girls' Romances (1969) in my best
Mad, Mad Modes for Moderns outfit
unwearable fashions on impossible cartoon models
rendered in pen-and-ink surreal *oh yeah* finery
right next to *Susan Says*
the advice column for distraught
thirteen-year-old girls whose boyfriends
are jealous of The Beatles and who tell them
they have to make a choice

But, Diane!
the square boy on the comic book cover pleads
hoping to lure her away from the groovy boy
she's dancing with at the swinging hot spot
I thought you were in love with me!
her purple shorts flash high thighs
the groovy boy's hand low at her hip
Grow up! she yells at the square over the din
her spangled bracelets clanking as she
pushes him away
You're yesterday, baby!

a trip to the Salvation Army store
takes care of it
floor-length vintage dress   purple paisley
pink swirls   long string of pearls
so fake they have seams
where the edges of the mould met

I buy a lime green handbag
very mod   I'll keep the stained
side toward me
no one will know
blue mascara and eye shadow
shimmery pink lip gloss and teased hair
a scarf (smelling
of mothballs) tied at my throat
a Mad Mad Modern *always* wears a scarf

The fab fashion of the year! The scarf's
splashed out! So get with it! Be IN
by going way-out with a swinging scarf!

a touch of fake Chanel No. 5 at my wrists
behind my ears   in my hair
spritz the teasing into place
there's a rumour you might be there
just wait till you get a look at me, Paul
the rest of those girls won't stand a chance
smooth my mad mod hair
I look just like Jane Asher
on her way to India with you

something big and real and gorgeous
is waiting in there for me

ii. You Don't Show

B.B. King   Hendrix   John and Yoko
at each new photo I take a quick
peek around in case
you snuck in
the museum guy keeps telling me you're not here
we stand together before a dimly lit
and sweating Jim Morrison
a young man moves behind me
carrying a Hofner violin bass guitar in his right hand

~

I guess I really didn't expect you, Paul
you've likely seen enough
of your wife's pictures of you
1971   frolicking
in Scotland with long-legged dogs

seen enough of this shot
you   naked
stretched out on a bed of potato boxes
and dusty blankets
your left hip exposed
gaze steaming   drowsy
new wife behind the camera
daughter across your thigh

iii. Tribute Band

Linda's vegetarian delicacies on long low tables
her photos of you on walls
wine spilled everywhere
fake hippies dancing   drinking   pretending
they don't have to go to work tomorrow
in banks and shoe stores

somebody announces the band
and a beautiful man in a silver Paul
suit grabs a guitar
from a stand on his way downstage
he sings the first notes of *I Saw Her Standing There*
the bass guitar natural in his hands

he plays right-handed!
every damn one of these fake Pauls
is right-handed
can't they find a left
-handed guy to play you?

he starts to sweat as soon as the light hits him
throat shining, a little swagger
kissing the microphone   a wink for the girls
he keeps his eyebrows raised like you did, Paul
my lips are dry   can't move
watch the guitar bounce
against his hip

~

god, Paul, this kid looks just like you
his hair   smiles   the way he tilts his head
churns his body against the Hofner
touch of Liverpool in his voice
did he see the resemblance to you
then learn to play your guitar?

he's got your eyes   and his lean thighs
stretch the grey silk when he dances
takes his deep rehearsed bows

at the first chords of *Day Tripper*
dancers abandon wineglasses
at the edge of the stage   his Cuban toes
kick them over as he comes
downstage to sing with fake George

a half dozen hippies
rush the stage drunk shouting
play 'Revolution'! play 'Let it Be'!
for godsakes the band is in
Love Me Do suits

I'll dance by myself at fake Paul's side
of the stage   never take my eyes from
him even when he's not singing
          there!   he winked at me
I didn't imagine that

iv. fake Paul Fantasy I

he and I are friends
he invites me to the show
to his dressing room
lets me watch him

in his white dress shirt and boxers
looking at himself in the mirror
he takes the wig from its white
eyeless styrofoam face
pulls it over his head
inside is sticky netting
sweat from last night's show
he tucks up his chestnut curls at the temples
tugs the wig over his forehead
to rest above his eyebrows
evens it up at his ears
pulls it easy at the back to just touch
his white collar
he bobby-pins the wig to his hair
holds the next pin between his lips

tonight it's the silver suit with the black
velvet collar   tapered lapels   silk
lining visible inside the cuffs
the early 1964 suit with a narrow black tie
he stands, pulls the slim legs of the tailored pants
over his thighs and hips
tucks in the white shirt
fastens the button   pulls the zipper

smoothes fabric either side
of his cock   slips his arms
into the jacket sleeves
shrugs his shoulders to settle it
on his thin frame
two red picks go into his right front pocket

someone announces the band   I hear
applause and shrieks
take my place in the wings
can't wait
to watch him play

v. Meet and Greet

I've bought him a beer
try not to let it get too warm in my hand
touch the edge of the rim
rub it on my wrist a little

the four of them sit at a table
smiling, signing other people's names
on studio shots   posed like Beatles
the glass of wine in my other hand
is almost gone   I hold back
till the others have had
their pictures taken   pumped his hand
spilled their wine on him

when it's my turn he thanks me
sips gratefully
I tell him I loved the show
he touches my arm
he's really looking at me
maybe he likes the scent of Chanel No. 5
maybe he thinks I'm nice

I talk my way backstage
he takes me through curtains and metal
rods to the green room
he grabs me a beer from the band's supply
another for himself
mirrors reflect suits on hangers
jeans and t-shirts slung over chairs

here's a shot of him all made up
a Polaroid showing proper skin tone
line of cheekbone
toss of that 1964 hair
a stray lock carefully placed
across his forehead

the way performers behave
in dressing rooms
is like you're not there
they just take off their John and George suits
in front of you without a thought
a lithe and moist fake George strolls around
in his underwear still
wearing his wig   soft-spoken
tells me about some freak at last week's show
who thought he *was* George
he tells me this girl
was crying in the front row
like that cute blonde in *A Hard Day's Night*
weeping, mouthing the name *George*

or the woman who'd received
his secret messages from the stage
and understood
said she'd never pursued a man like him before
her husband and kids were away all week
she wrote
sent him her address

the fake Paul kid
(still in his McCartney suit and hair)
is showing me pictures
his four-year-old son
sandwiched between teddy bears at
Sears   I make all the right noises
sit in his chair
sip my beer, watch him

take off the suit jacket
hang it on the rack
pockets of sweat under his arms
across his shoulders
thin cotton underneath   the expensive
fabric clings to his body with sweat
outlining a jut of rib
dark hard nipple visible when he
reaches to loosen his tie
I see pale skin above
the tight waistband
he turns from me for a moment
takes off the shirt   smooth
thin back still shining
shoulder blades and spine turning
he slides into
a David Bowie t-shirt

I haven't seen his hair yet
he's shy to take off his wig in front of me

The Players' Club
[Off-Track Betting Room and Casino, Camrose, Alberta. Winter]

I'm the fifth fucking Beatle!
the belligerent drunk screams
clinking bottles of Pilsner
the other guy in a red baseball hat
away from the wife tonight not expecting
a fake Beatles band at his favourite watering hole
they've turned off the jukebox
all the country songs he loves
so these pussies can put on fake hair
and play that shit sixties crap

the drunks order another round
from a tired-looking waitress called Michelle
her sticky tray lifted over bad comb-overs and
big hair sprayed in place   curling smoke from
cigarettes at every mouth

after the encore
they enter the crowd in character
sign their names   shake
hands   turn down propositions from the bored drunk
housewife on her weekly night out with the girls
she staggers Beatle to Beatle hoping
one of them will take her up on it
they smile   hold her
from their bodies
she wouldn't recognize them
if they passed her on the street
without wigs without
jackets, ties, Beatle boots

a full beer is slammed
on a terry towel table cloth
fresh Pilsner releases the stench
of all the Pilsners spilled before it
the cover frayed and full of cigarette holes

fake Paul nods   answers the woman's stupid
questions   his hands
clasped now behind his back
is he really from Liverpool?
she's not the first to ask
his answer a quiet thank you for
the compliment about his accent

he is looking for me
a stray bit of wig
sweat damp and clinging
to his brow   those big eyes apologetic
we can talk soon   let me get rid of
this one and we can talk

the fifth Beatle rises
two Pilsners fall to the sticky carpet
roll to the drain at the centre
of the fake wood dance floor
clink together like old lovers waltzing
the man weaves to the bandstand
pushes the woman aside   reaches
toward fake Paul's head
the wig comes off in his hand inside out
bobby pins pull out hair
the man slaps the brown hunk
on his baseball cap
drunken air guitar for a second or two
before fake Paul snatches it back
leaves for the dressing room without a word

fake Paul Fantasy II

ten-by-ten makeshift dressing room
a door that won't close
he paces   the wig in his hands

I knock on a flimsy wall
he pulls me in
arms around my neck   wig
at my cheek

it smells of him
I pull away   take the wig
gentle from his hands
I can fix it
where's his brush?
where's that styrofoam head?

he brings me the things I need
opens two Coronas
watches me touch
the damaged hair   the wig inside out
where I've placed it netting side up on the head
feeling for bobby pins
he leans in   shoulder touching mine
he places the fingers of his right hand
at the base of the squeaky neck
his left hand touches mine as he holds
the wig in place for me

I turn it over   mould it to the white head
sightless feminine eyes stare past me
it looks odd wearing this masculine hair

I pull his own curls from the brush first   flutter them
from my fingers to the concrete floor
I work from the crown forward
part it at his left
brush the bangs to his right
my hand touches his as I move it down
to hold the netting under the wet strands
just enough stray curl in front to play at his eyebrow
now the hair at the temples
straight down to cover the top of his ears
I know what I'm doing

he moves his hand
from the head to my neck   slides it
under my long hair
my brush working through black strands
his fingers are cool   I put the brush down
he's watching me   his right hand
on my skin   left cradling his own jaw
he's forgotten the wig though I'm not
finished with it

fingers tangle themselves
in the hair at the nape of my neck
his breath closer
grow bold   dare to play with it a little
shape it with my hands
I know how this curl should look
he's moved my hair from my face
take the lick of
bangs between my left thumb and forefinger
shape it just the way I like
his lips at my throat
my hands steady on black
layers at the neck

Put Your Guitar Down

he looks so blue
that big hazel faraway look
fake George's Fender Stratocaster gently weeps
him upstage   into the background
into his steady bass beat
corners of his full mouth turned down

the second before and after this
one   a joyous grin   a Paul
smile   high eyebrows   lots of teeth
tilting hips   all the Paul sway
his crowd swaying with him

the wig tight and uncomfortable
this late in the show   eyes tired
he is so tired
makeup dripping into his collar
jawbone set

is he thinking of his boy?
is this how he imagined it would be?
travelling in cold vans for hours
playing Paul in small
town bars must suck
the very life from him
must take everything he's got
to get up there night after night
be someone he's not in smoky pubs
for people who mostly don't give a shit
late nights full with haze   old beer
drunken losers belching song
titles at him when he had dreamed
more for himself   for his son

put your guitar down
I will hold my arms out to you

fake Paul

I imagine he watches me
from makeshift bandstands
hugs me on dance floors after dripping
gigs in bored casinos and shabby nightclubs
orange terry towel on small round tables
spilled beer   a bar fight just outside a winter door

he doesn't fool me, Paul
though he seems nice and polite
quick to say hello to me
in front of everyone
the first to offer me a beer
a place to sit backstage

what is it about me he likes?
is he turned on because he knows
he's as close as I'll ever get to you?
maybe he feels like you when I'm around
maybe he's guessed what I do
to myself
in rooms next to his
how I listen for him moving
into bed   sighing into sleep
how my blood soaks through cheap cotton sheets
into saggy hotel mattresses
how I lie there in it, cold, till morning

Show the Next Night

[Elementary School Fundraiser, Varscona Hotel Ballroom, Whyte Avenue, Edmonton]

i. Michelle

I get there late on purpose
don't want to seem too eager

he sees me   says hello
to me in his microphone in front of
everyone   he says it's good to see a friend
he called me *a friend*
all the madeup fundraiser women look at me
I bet they're jealous I know the band

when he's not singing he steals
glances at me
makes sure I'm watching his
thin fingers   the strings pulsing

now he asks if anyone is called Michelle
I could fucking be Michelle
a frumpy woman with grease
in her hair calls, *I'm Michelle!*

she's not even looking at him
she's talking to her friends while he sings
                    to her!
he doesn't even look at me the whole song
I'll tell him I broke the wineglass accidentally
cut myself a bit but I'm all right
leave my blood on the table

I can see the veins in his throat at the high notes
singing in French to an ugly woman who
couldn't care less

ii. drunk women tugging

after the second set, fake Paul grows bold
jumps from the stage
puts a light arm around my shoulders
good to see you again
I turn into him and my hands sink into silk
wet and warm at his back

so high on him
a sweet scent from
under his arms
he leaves a slick film on my skin
squeezes me on this dance floor
hands on my back
breath on my throat

drunk women tug at his sleeves
fondle his ass
he has to go be charming now
he has to go be *Paul*
their hands are on me too
fake nails tangled in my hair
they try to pull me off him

they've been throwing themselves all
over him   it's disgusting
climbing on stage all night
dancing with him   rubbing themselves
against him   drunk

idiots
it's not the *real* him
anyone can see that
screaming like he's Paul
as if they love him
I know they don't
not like I do

I hold him tighter
crush my pelvis into his
lift handfuls of suit in my fists
he stiffens   reaches behind himself
pulls my hands from his waist
I whisper *I've always loved you*

the stage manager takes me
by the shoulder   *that's enough now*
a low voice in my ear
blond curls at my cheek
pulls me away   gentle
thanks, Damien he says
he's looking at me
wrong   backing away
what's the matter with him?
I was just in his room the other night!

iii. guitar bouncing light

what he's left me dries on my throat
I watch him walk to the bar
grab his beer   let it slip
past his Adam's apple
a small swallow and *ah*
his bottom lip collects the foam
he looks toward me
where I'm standing in the centre of the floor
I'm here, baby
waiting for you
holding out my still-wet hands
he looks away when I
catch his eye

watching him
the room moving past me
in glittered up-dos and painted lips
I see it all so clearly
our life together
our babies and home   babies with
eyes like his   a bungalow in a wooded
valley subdivision   room for the kids
and sheepdog
I feel sure he must want one

I see how his body would cover mine
he would finish playing me a song, lay the guitar
on the carpet at his feet
he would rest his right hand on my knee
his eyes would be open while he touched me
just don't say anything   don't say anything
you won't sound like Paul
his mouth over mine
I'd ask him to leave the wig on

lift my face and let the glass
disco-ball squares stab my eyes
grab a chair near me for balance

I hang back   watch
his hand over hair
I know it *isn't* his hair
he leans, one Beatle boot up on the bar rail
sipping his beer and smiling
at the ridiculous women
talking to them   nodding   winking
their hands all over him   breasts
against the wet
of his suit
their breath hot in his ear
fake John pulls him away
rescues him from their drooling mouths
back to the bandstand

I turn away from the stage
across from the dance floor the walls
are covered in mirrors
floor to ceiling
catch you in one   your guitar bouncing
light   it is you
your Hofner pointed the right way now
I knew it was you all along

you start playing *You Can't Do That*
I stumble through bodies
tripping on high heels and sick
on the hot stink of perfume
I see the dressing room to my left

No Admittance   Rubber Soul Only
I don't look back   duck into
the little room   I can
breathe in here
baseball-sized bulbs surround the mirror
everything is blue and bright
a photo of you taped up
the way I saw it before
I'll leave the Scotch tape on the mirror
next to your mates' snapshots

your brush on the counter
I sit in your blue makeup chair
pull your hair from the bristles
drag it across my
open eyes
slice my corneas
with black strands

iv. Pick

I know where this has been
night after night   held
between the calloused thumb
and index finger of your right hand
the pick so worn on both sides
I can't read the name

maybe you carry it
in your front pocket
before every gig
maybe it gets hot next to your thigh
while you dress
warm up your voice
blend makeup and powder

pots and brushes laid out
car keys on the counter
I finger kids' pictures   wedding rings
throw them back on the smooth surface

I sit in your chair
lean over   inhale
the smell of powder and sweat
it takes some doing
I scrape away
I Should Have Known Better
bass line pounds in my head
soon, here are a few drops
(the pick edge not as sharp as I thought)
hold my left wrist over
the picture of you
    pinch
with my right thumb and index finger
skin either side of the vein

v. I'll lean on the bar casually

when I come out
you're just finishing your set
I reach up   smooth my hair loosened
by the effort of showing my
love for you   dragging
dull plastic across a blue vein

I can see the door from here
you pop in
come out looking apprehensive
you might still be thirsty   you work
hard up there
I'll ask if I can buy you a beer

you don't come to the bar
I hide my arm behind my back

you scan the room for
John probably or George
not Ringo
he's way too busy packing up drums
to notice you

now you talk to a security guard
you see me! point at me
John joins you, one hand on his hip
the other at your back
you're both looking at me
blood from my hand drips on the floor
I hope I'm not staining my new dress
feel a splash along my ankle

vi. Smear

I pose beside the bar
a glass of white in my right hand
a drop of red swirls on top
pools at the centre

my left elbow is draped
across the bar, fingers still dripping
you're on the dance floor with John
the security guy is walking over
he grabs my wine arm
it spills! *watch it buddy*

they make me leave my wine at the bar
it was expensive too
he hauls me across the floor
in front of everyone   in front of you
I give you a wink as I pass
John's arm across your chest
the security guy drags me into the *No
Admittance   Rubber Soul Only* room
damage control
someone has put on *Run for Your Life*
it echoes over the din of voices
they're turning the lights up
women try to find their purses
will this goon let me go?
I need to talk to you

he turns on the big round lights
mirrors slashed with red
I Love You Paul!!
fingertip-shaped drops smoking on bulbs
blood kisses on glass

my forehead smeared red
where I tried to fix my hair
it's not too bad
I'll try again with my free hand

Jostled by the Street Crowd

a back door opens and I'm tossed into the alley   a bag of
    garbage to be picked up in the morning
thugs' faces surge above me one's bow tie a little crooked
    why should I go quietly?
I've got as much right as   anyone to be here
I bought my fucking ticket like everybody else

there's dirt in my wrists I'm on my hands and knees
rocks and blood on my dress
these goons won't see me cry   bastards

    Paul?

some drunk bitch walks on my
hand with her fucking shoe
my cuts are filled with rocks

the men slammed the door behind them
no handle on the outside I can't get back in
covered in mud and rain
dirty footprint leftovers I am caught
in the gush of bodies   lifted by unseen hands
    are you okay? yeah yeah yeah
shake off the hot hands   knocked
over again another drunk lunatic
group their faces a fun house mirror nightmare of stretched and
    twisted mouths vicious laughing
teeth I hit a wall of boozy smoke lights pulse feet pulse
past me music pulses from inside my
skull   my wrists drip on
pavement   a man jostles me sends me sideways
into the push and stench of bodies and lights

I'm covered in mud
lost a shoe and the night pours on around me slushy with
light and music
      food smells vomit and fucking in doorways

I stumble to my hotel room
my room next to his   my blood next to his
leave a handprint in blood and pebbles on his door
I'll clean up   find him in the morning
find him tomorrow

Concert

A Paul Dream Last Night

[Hippodrome Theatre, Birmingham, 10 November 1963]

walk through cool air
closed shops, barred windows
a mannequin in ermine
watches me pass
her hairless head squeaks on her neck
empty eyes follow me
I arrive at Hurst Street
find my way backstage

Paul, you sit, legs crossed
on a black leather couch
a cigarette in your left hand
look up from your newspaper
watch me walk into the room
the radio DJ there holds a microphone
steers me toward you
explains the rules
he tells you I'm wearing an
exciting new perfume
one you might like
if you can guess what it is, you win

you crush your cigarette
in the ashtray on the side table
lift your body
place your right hand flat
against the bone above my left breast
your paper falls to the floor
you brush my skin with your lashes
now your mouth at my throat
breathe through your nose
catch my scent

you wear a new black suit
mop-top against my cheek
one hand touches me moving slightly
the other at my waist
you go on in a few minutes

you are trying to guess but you
need to collect more of my smell
need to move closer
touch me

my breath all ragged
your ear so close to my mouth
I say nothing
release me
you win

Seventeenth Floor Window

[Royal York Hotel, Toronto, Ontario
5:00 p.m., 13 April 2002]

you are somewhere near me now
doing a sound check or
eating supper
I've waited all my life for you
I'm ready   unpacked all my things
my bits of leaves   wax hand and your head
some money and a pick

we are in the same city
tonight we'll be in the same room
swirling in the arena-stink of people who couldn't
love you half as much as I do

I don't have a ticket
stand at the window
on the seventeenth floor
I can see the stadium from here
your red tour trucks lined up outside
security people and staff come and go

I should sit down while I do this
drag the round table over to the window
suppose I'll have to pay
for the broken water glass
I don't have time to do it with the pick
I stole from fake Paul
lift a few drops to my wrists
cover the cuts with the band-aids I brought
I'll tell them to put it on my bill
don't want to pay
to have the carpet
cleaned too

sway back and forth
a little movement
rain on my window   the light is fading
a limo pulls around back of the arena
chased by grown women
faces running with mascara

Ticket

it won't be easy getting past them
not with all this stuff
but a glance through my backpack
and I'm in   already weeping
it always works
nobody wants
to search a crying woman

I hold my arms up without being asked
the security guy wands me
but I'm not worried
what I'm carrying doesn't beep
I have only your head with me
don't want to be bogged down
fake Paul's pick makes it through
with me no problem

bought this ticket from a scalper
I was a hundred short but
he gave it to me for two fifty plus
I sucked him off real fast behind the tour trucks

give my ticket to someone to rip
find my seat in the front row

Littleboy Red Shirt

Hofner bass pounds
grinding you two and a half hours
vibration and rub

sticky love and flowers pelt your
thighs your mouth
you smash them as you play
the scent of bruised roses and crushed bodies
drowns me

my front row arms tingle and ache
hands   throat   heart raw caught in the bass
line swelter and pump
Can't Buy Me Love
I dig the pick into my throat
offer myself to you
beer and blood mix at my feet

fingers   slippery British wrists
blow me a kiss
take me home
littleboy red shirt   tight jeans
I feel your tongue in my mouth
you pour into me hard

don't fight me
it's meant to be
don't fight me

your eyes find me
I feel a baby move into me
I crash to my knees as she takes hold
she is yours and mine

outside
a hotel limo pulls you away from me
before the arena lights are up

turn my face to the little rain falling

Voice after the show

outside in the tug and push
of crying sated bodies
a voice calls
tells me it might be hard
carrying this child to term
I hold both hands over my belly and listen

remember when you were
a little girl? the voice asks
yes I do
her voice is above me all around me
bodies brush past, rain falling
my backpack is heavy
and you loved him
more than anyone?
yes, I remember
now that you're all grown up, she says,
don't let anyone take that away
he belongs to you   you and our baby
he'll never belong to anyone else

she was killed waiting
to see you in New York City a long time ago
she wanted to tell you about the baby
Ed Sullivan was safe inside the studio
and you never knew
her baby born dead in the street
her best blue sweater ruined by blood

lying in the street
she turned her head as girls
stomped over her belly
she turned her head
to see where they were going
across the street at the appliance store
girls slammed into the glass
pushed against it from behind
kisses against the window

six television sets full with your face
the young woman watched though she couldn't
always see you through the bouncing heads
girls in winter parkas
frenzied girls who couldn't get in
mittens thudding on windows
screams condensing on dirty glass

Collection
[11:48 p.m., Royal York Hotel]

your head   torn ticket
these strands of black hair
from fake Paul's wig
that sweet thing who was you
for a moment
my dress bloody at the hem
knife   his pick
wax hand
our baby kicking inside me
decaying suit jacket   fibreglass
a few drops of my blood

lay you on my bed
build up your body with
sheets and pillows
stuff pillowcases into the arms of your jacket
you look kind of lumpy   not too bad
I put leaves from the tree outside
your house at your wrists
this unravelling grey jacket
over your shoulders
buttoned to your throat
your head at the jacket's neck
shape the fingers of your wax
left hand around his pick
smooth your hair
do you want a sip of my wine?

you look nice all dressed up
but a little uncomfortable
I'll undo these buttons for you

114

you're looking straight up
do you see us
in the big mirror over our heads?
we look so good together
warm you in my hands
carve the magic word
into your forehead with the edge
of my thumbnail
breathe into your mouth
I love you
bring you to life

She's Yours Too

she moves in me   a little kick
I pull your wax left hand
from its cuff
hold it to my belly
do you feel her?
she's yours too
naturally you'll want a relationship
with her   I won't stop you
from being her father

she'll be better off with you anyways
all those horses, dogs, fancy cars
she will grow up in your big house
run around all day and never
see the same room twice
that's how I imagine your house
that's how I imagine her in your house

she waits for you to come out
leave the studio in your London home
to play with her
she is five or six
old enough to love
young enough not to understand
who you are
she will grow to wish
she'd been there in the early days
seen you at the Cavern
wanting you from that hot vantage point
on the verge of the stardom
she does not yet recognize

you'll love her
like you secretly love me
you haven't always, it's true
but you're here now
listening to every word I say
all dressed up lying
down with me on a hotel bedspread
I watch us in the big mirror
my hands unzipping you
unbuttoning you   my thigh across yours
we would make such a nice family
she will see every day how much
her parents love each other
and won't she laugh when she hears
the story of how we made her!

on the hotel room TV, a rerun
of *The Ed Sullivan Show*
from February 9th, 1964
All My Loving   how my mother
loved that song
loved you
you are watching *me* now, not her

You'll Burn for Me

kiss your lips
your cheeks   gnaw on your earlobes
bite off your left ear   suck it into me
suck eyeballs and hair follicles
gasp for breath
swallow you   take you inside me
you and our baby both inside me now
your own voice from the television

in my pocket I find
the lighter I held up
when you sang *Let it Be*

you'll burn for me
cotton and wax and hair
burn for me, lover
smear the magic from your forehead
you'll return to me
I'll return you to the wax

builds up in me
no need for breath
so full of you my love
I float toward the diamond light

Coda

brown leather jacket loose
at his shoulders, Jim wipes his
fingerprints from the face
of the Gretsch Tennessean he's owned
for eighteen years he has
packed the guitar in velvet
snapped the clasps on the worn
case with one hand, raised a Heineken
to his mouth with the other

stepping over stray cords   two
in the morning   humming 'It's All Too Much'
Jim digs his knuckles into watery eyes
bends to pick up a cord
coils it elbow to palm   elbow to palm
runs his other hand through
short hair free of the George wig
runners have replaced Beatle boots

he gives Rob a hand loading
the keyboard into the van
their breath follows them through dark air
at the back door
the van running   guitars   Vox amps
boxes of drumsticks and tambourines
Rob tells Jim, "you murdered that solo
tonight, man. It was great."

Damien unplugs amplifiers
curly blond hair shaken out
his tamborines and guitar cases at his feet
his acoustic waits at the door
it will go in last
come into his motel room with him
Gary might pick it up later
if he can't sleep   if he wants
to play 'Blackbird'

from the basement dressing room
Gary and Keith carry five
garment bags between them

each holds:

one grey suit with a collarless jacket
two white cotton dress shirts
smoke of a hundred cigarettes
a black silk suit
another of silver with a velvet collar
two pairs of black socks
the long night's music and love
one thin black tie
a pair of Beatle boots

wigs in boxes ride inside a larger box
tossed into the van on top of a black case
holding Gary's Hofner bass guitar
Gary, shivering in a thin
grey leather coat, slides
into the driver's seat
revs the engine to keep it from stalling
the last of Keith's drums are packed up
the band waits on cold vinyl
exhausted, impatient
Gary walks back into the bar
hazel eyes bright in the fluorescent
skin of old smoke   chairs tipped
upside down on tables
his boots make hardly a sound
on the worn black wood
he takes a last look onstage for anything
he may have left behind

Acknowledgements

my deepest thanks and love to my husband Stu for thoughtful reading of these poems, for attending a zillion *Rubber Soul* concerts, for sending me to Liverpool with a kiss, and for sticking with me all these years despite The Paul McCartney Thing. you knew what you were getting into when you married me, baby.

many, many thanks to Todd, Sharon, Manservant Kelly, and Pat at Turnstone Press.

thanks to my sister Karen for channelling me and ripping the sign off Paul McCartney's dressing room door at the Liverpool Cathedral Church of Christ, and for buying me a ticket to the *Linda McCartney's Sixties* photo exhibition as a birthday gift.

my heartfelt thanks to Gary Boylan, the sweet guy who used to play Paul in *Rubber Soul: the Canadian Tribute*. thank you for inspiring this book that night, for very generously talking with me about what it's like to be you, for continued friendship, for reading my poems with care and sensitivity, and for offering to see me safely to my car late one night after a *Rubber Soul* show. Gary, you are a true gentleman and a gifted musician.

for years of faithful editing, fine wine and friendship, and for the odd well-timed exclamation of *Holy Shit!* many thanks and much love to: Bert Almon, Holly Borgerson Calder, Rebecca Campbell, Lori Claerhout, Olga Costopoulos, Joan Crate, Dave Elias, Lee Elliott, Heidi Greco, Leslie Greentree, Catherine Greenwood, Shawna Lemay, Iman Mersal, Blaine Newton, and Michael Penny. J, B, and especially L: all my best wine and cheese to you for the EFPR. I so owe you one.

much love and many thanks to the former members of my very own rock band, *Rubber Soul: the Canadian Tribute.* you lads rocked my world so hard. my thanks to Jim Harrison (*George*), Damien Johnson (*the fifth Beatle*), Rob Mackroth (*John*), Keith McTaggart (*Ringo*), and former band manager Greg Gazin. thanks also to Rich Crooks and Steve Nixon. every girl should have her very own rock band at least once in her life. I'm glad you were mine.

my thanks and affection to Paul Wharton in St. Helens, Merseyside, for showing me the Liverpool tourists never get to see, for your patience in teaching me the nuances of Scouse, for giving me *Blood Brothers*, the writing garden at the Bluecoat, and Rab MacRab. ta very much, la. you're a cracking bloke.

many thanks to Cath Nichols, Chris Clarke, and the Dead Good Poets Society, Liverpool, for allowing me to read my work and for being kind and gracious toward me. thanks to my fellow readers that night: Julian, Nick, and Peter Finch. thanks to the Everyman Bistro in Hope Street, Liverpool. thanks as well to Paul's mates for the welcome and the fun, especially Jackie, Laura, and Alan.

thanks to my editor, Dennis Cooley, and to the late Manuela Dias for taking a chance on me all those years ago. thanks to Paul, Terry, Lee, and *The Deluxe Lounge*. many thanks, as always, to St. Peter's Abbey and especially to Father Demetrius, who can find me a room and a job at a moment's notice. thanks to Terry Rahbek-Nielsen, Mark Tovey, Susan A.S. Wilson, and to Macca-L and the Toronto *Paul Crawl* gang.

love and thanks to my families and friends, and especially to my godson Griffin "Sledgehammer" Cork, and to my goddaughters Ella Johnson for being the greatest Christmas gift ever, and Jalesa Briault for sharing *Rubber Soul* with me and for keeping Uncle Stu company while I wrote this book.

thank you for everything, real Paul.

some of these poems have appeared, in slightly different form, in *CV2*, *grain*, and *JONES AV*. my thanks to the editors. the quotes in "Mad, Mad Modes for Moderns" are from *The Revealing Secrets of Girls' Romances,* No. 144, October 1969, National Periodical Publications Inc, Sparta, Illinois. I owe much of the imagery in "Oily Lace" to the "Eleanor Rigby" segment of *Yellow Submarine*. the cover image of Gary Boylan as Paul McCartney is by Greg Gazin. it is reprinted by permission.

"Underground: at The Beatles Story Museum, Albert Dock" is for Rebecca Campbell. "Sound Check" is for Holly Borgerson Calder. "Behind the Cavern, 2:00 a.m., 04 August 1963" is for Susan Wilson. "20 Forthlin Road" is for Paul Wharton. "knapsack" is for Catherine Greenwood. "Opening Night: *Linda McCartney's Sixties* Photo Exhibition" is for Karen Johnson-Diamond Cork. "I'll lean on the bar casually" is for Leslie Greentree. "Littleboy Red Shirt" is for Mark Tovey. "You'll Burn for Me" is for Heidi Greco. "Coda" is for Stu.